The Curator of Silence

THE ERNEST SANDEEN PRIZE IN POETRY

EDITOR

John Matthias

2007, *The Curator of Silence*, Jude Nutter

2005, *Lives of the Sleepers*, Ned Balbo

2003, *Breeze*, John Latta

2001, *No Messages*, Robert Hahn

1999, *The Green Tuxedo*, Janet Holmes

1997, *True North*, Stephanice Strickland

The CURATOR of SILENCE

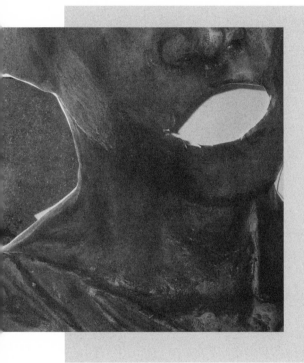

JUDE NUTTER

University of Notre Dame Press

Notre Dame, Indiana

Published by the University of Notre Dame Press
Notre Dame, Indiana 46556
www.undpress.nd.edu

Manufactured in the United States of America

Reprinted in 2007, 2008

Library of Congress Cataloging-in-Publication Data

Nutter, Jude.
The curator of silence / Jude Nutter.
p.   cm. — (The Ernest Sandeen prize in poetry ; 2007)
Poems.
ISBN-13: 978-0-268-03661-4 (pbk. : alk. paper)
ISBN-10: 0-268-03661-6 (pbk. : alk. paper)
I. Title.
PS3614.U884C87 2006
811'.6—dc22

2006023894

∞ *The paper in this book meets the guidelines for permanence and durability*
of the Committee on Production Guidelines for Book Longevity of the Council on
Library Resources.

for my family,

as always

Contents

Acknowledgments

Grateful acknowledgment is made to the following journals in which some of these poems, or earlier versions of them, first appeared:

Chautauqua Literary Journal: "Aurelia aurita"
Gulf Coast: "Permission"
MARGIE: The American Journal of Poetry: "The Fourth Man," "Boys Throwing Baseball"
Missouri Review: "The Last Supper," "To the Reader," "The Rest of Us," "Horses"
Notre Dame Review: "Grave Robbing with Rilke"
Post Road: "The Dream in Broad Daylight," "Elegy for Mumbai"
Tor House Newsletter: "The Hermit Thrush"
Water-Stone: "The Cherry Picker," "One Year of Not Drinking: A Letter at Thanksgiving"
Words and Images: "Crow"

"The Last Supper," "Horses," "To the Reader" and "The Rest of Us" won the 2004 Larry Levis Prize awarded by the *Missouri Review.* "Boys Throwing Baseball" won the 2002 Margery J. Wilson Award awarded by *MARGIE: The American Journal of Poetry.* "One Year of Not Drinking: A Letter at Thanksgiving" won the Loft's 2002 National Prize in Poetry. "The Hermit Thrush" won the 2001 Robinson Jeffers Tor House Prize.

To the Reader

Out here, in darkness, rain knocks
against the earth, unlocking tiny doors
in the dirt of the garden. You
have spent your whole life so far
trying to bear your body as a blessing,
and now you are waiting with your empty
suitcase between your father's
toolshed and the high, rough fence
of the neighbours' garden, and whatever

it is the rain sets free from the soil it tastes
like the vacancy of the grave, it tastes
like the hunger you discovered
when you entered this world—released
from the grip of your mother's body and passed,
fully condemned, into the slack cage
of your father's arms: the brand-new loneliness
of the body you'd been given. This
emptiness is the only thing you have

that will always belong to you. In the bone-
thin light of her kitchen your mother
is singing, but you can't hear it. You watch
as her red mouth opens like a wound. And closes.
She looks like a butcher in her shiny apron, shaving
the skins from the carrots and potatoes.
You want her to leave the peels stacked up

like scrolls on the counter and walk out
into the rain in her new slippers; you want
her to crawl, weeping, on her knees in darkness,
turning every stone in the garden and parting
the tall stems of the hollyhocks, weeping
and calling your name. You want her to believe
you are lost. Like one of the dead. Just once

1

would mean everything. And be enough.
You were born, your mother once said, *in darkness,*
before dawn—she remembers the milkman
whistling up the drive, the scraping of bottles
on the grit of the top step; that your father was busy
down in the garden digging a hole
in which he will set your placenta
and a sapling that will later grow waxy,
long-throated blossoms no one can name.
Even in summer those flowers will fill
with shadow and not once will the bees ever enter
their slick hallways. Soon, you will go inside

and say nothing, and your mother
will go on believing the appetite you have is literal.
You came into this world, she once said,
without a single sound. There's a prayer
we send out, in darkness, toward darkness.
And your heart, out of habit, keeps on
saying it: *Mother,* it whispers, *mother, mother.*
Meaning: my jailer and my liberator. *I never*
really worried, your mother will tell you
years from now; *I always knew*
you'd come home when you were hungry.

Meaning: I'm not sure how to love you now
that I have turned you loose
from the prison of my body and into
this greater, and less literal darkness.

Permission

An egg, after all, is a beautiful thing long
before it's a metaphor for the perils of this world,
so how this is meant to dissuade
them from sex, or even love, is a mystery, and yet
they sashay through the halls all day with their small burdens,
which they wrap in scarves and T-shirts, and pack,
in pairs, inside baskets and tins. *A broken egg,*

they are told, *means a broken child,* even though,
in real life, the body is more durable
than we dare to think. So this
is the burden of the future, and who
among them is truly equipped to bear it.
Imagine, I say, what it might be like
inside an egg, and they picture rooms shut tight
against the weather—outside, rain
and wind with such distance
inside their talking. *Surely*, someone argues,
a broken egg's more fitting since the future is mostly

emptiness and loss, and I
want to tell them how my mother
once took me out to the barn and lifted,
from that golden curdle beneath the heat lamps,
a single chick, which she placed in my palm
so I might discover, when it mattered most,
that an egg weighs more than the small
bird breaking from it. If this would help them,
I can't say, but I know a burden
need never be as heavy as we first believe.
But they care so little for the past, and because
the future is, mostly, emptiness and loss, we hike
to the wooded border of the playing field
where the jackdaws nest, where they place down

and so forget their baskets and tins, searching
instead for the empty eggs, tipped from the nest
and scattered like tiny, overturned buckets
among the shepherd's purse and the vetch.

It begins to rain. In the buildings across the field
someone is flicking lights on against the storm.
Tins and baskets lie abandoned
in the grass and the jackdaws are calling *loss, loss,*
from the high, green darkness of the beeches;
and there, beneath them, a girl
and a boy stand waiting inside the noise of the falling rain:
she has noticed how the small flies gather
beneath the trees in a storm because she is looking
upward and pointing toward the green
undercarriage of leaves; and this boy, who has waited
longer than even he can remember, moves

up behind her to lift, and then place his lips against,
the tip of her long, dark braid. And it was Proust,
wasn't it, who implored us to remember
that a kiss is the one thing that gives the heart leave
to accompany the body forward. It's gestures
like this that win the attention of the gods.
But still it might not save them:
think of how the hopeful and the hopeless alike
no doubt kiss, for luck, before ascending, the first rung

of the ladder that will take them closer to heaven.

The Hermit Thrush

The serpentine curves of the pine branches at upper left create
a sense of equivalence to the punctuated calls of the bird,
which we are given to imagine. . . .

— from exhibit notes for
Thomas Wilmer Dewing's
The Hermit Thrush

Because the heart asks only that we vanish
into the mystery beyond itself, you
have placed your bird beyond
the limits of the picture, where it remains known

solely by its absence. The miracle is how
you found equivalents for the silence arriving
after the rapid skirls of one bird singing:
a solitude so explicit we envy
the dead the world they inherit. And those

women you brought with you through the chrome
of twilight, we want them to kiss and undress
in the grass and make love to each other because
through the taunting haze of undergrowth you have woven

a marvelous, strapless longing and along
their arms wrestled down a light so solid it suggests
that they might well hold one another.
Even though we gather the world
to us in so many ways, most times, sex
is not one of them. The silence after

a bird stops singing is just the beginning
of a question we must imagine to completion.
And that woman in the olive-green dress is standing

now to meet it with her face upturned and her mouth
obscured behind a smudge of shadow: the evidence,
perhaps, of her own voice, which you have rendered
as the Rorschach of memory. O,

how much faith we must have
in the visible world: we move inside it
and come no closer. We follow her gaze to the white edge
of the page beneath our hands and, beyond this,
into the rooms where we are sitting,
with their relics of personal history, with their views

of the world in which we attempt our living.
And what of that world? Crows
fussing in the cottonwoods, brandishing
their fingered wings like dark gloves: the forgotten
accessories of minor angels who navigated

with us for years through the perils of illness
and traffic, and then grew tired; who left us
to the ruins of our own salvation.
This world, not as we see it, but as it is.
Where the heart travels, with us
for its own sake.

Grave Robbing with Rilke

You want to write about life
but you keep coming back to the body;
back to this untended, overgrown graveyard
where your small family mausoleum
has been broken open and the bone
ware of your parents' tomb keeps passing
out of one world and into another.

Even if god is something
in which you cannot believe, you need
to believe your dead remain
in one piece forever, and yet your parents
will not stop trading their earthly possessions:

you've seen them taken—clamped
in the jaws of the badger and the fox; carried
by the raven's mussel-black devices
toward an intention even you would call
heaven; and once, you found a darkness
of children, slick as stones in the rain,
waiting, as the one boy willing
to touch the dead for them all stepped forward
into the tomb and came back

with pieces of your parents in the basket
of his fingers. Any fall toward knowledge is won
through disobedience to the gods,
and as you watched him go—little hero,
with his pockets full of trinkets belonging to you—
you thought about Rilke, who claimed his god
was a dark god—*a webbing,* he said,
made of a hundred roots that drink in silence:

a metaphor, yes, but each metaphor reveals
the ghost of a literal world; and what acts
of desecration he must have committed
in order to claim it. He had his burden, and not once

did you think of calling that young boy back.
So you stand now in sunlight, on the splintered
threshold of your parents' grave, looking in:
and this, you tell yourself, *is how it must
have been for them when they stood,
in silence, in that brightly lit hallway just outside
the doorway to my room, watching
the rungs of my small ribs rising and falling.*

The Falcon

Justice and mercy
Are human dreams. . . .
— Robinson Jeffers

The falcon held motionless. At eye level.
Inside the wind. I stood at the edge
of a continent above a steep slope of gravel and scrub.
The water below and beyond. I heard
the level, bright tracks the wind followed in, steadily,
from the north. The keenings of its many mouths
across the bare rocks of the headland.
After it collapsed its wings and vanished
into the scrub, that bird then rode the wind
right back up to where it had been.
As if a shelf had been worn in the air
by its purpose. In its claws, a compact darkness,
a tail like a loose thread—a little body
at the apex of its terror. Then a sudden, brilliant
explosion of blood.
Which held in the air for the briefest moment.
Which was torn away on the wind. A pink mist.
Then nothing. The beauty
of it caught me by surprise. And what was left.
Against the constant shoveling of the wind
a slim bird, hanging. Its solitude and indifference.
The wind panicking in the hood of my jacket.
Around the rocks, collars of surf like spun glass.
The mind searching for the comfort
of metaphor. But why make it something
less than it was: a body,
emptied out, then a tiny heart clamping hard
around nothing.

The Garden Party

We spend our whole lives preparing
to lose each other. We are never ready.
On the headland every bench that faces
west is inscribed to someone's memory,
and how fitting it is to lean back all
afternoon against the names of the dead
and remember we never love anything
deep enough to hold it in this world. And yet
how beautiful for those on the deck of a boat
rounding the headland at evening—that litany
of small plaques hoarding the light.
It is easy to see why the dead move
westward, over water, toward
that slim whine of radiance along the horizon
where the buildings of some great city
are forever burning, resplendent
not with flame but with the echoes of bells
and singing—the brazen seduction
we have come to call heaven. Sit here

looking west, toward the horizon's
false promise of passage, and imagine
how the dead must feel, straddling
that gap between the deck of a boat
and the jetty with one foot in midair and the other
still in this world, as the captain
reaches his hand out to help them
over the gunwale. Imagine the bark
of gravel and grit beneath the sole
of a shoe as a body pushes forward, over
its fulcrum, onto a boat deck slick with spray;
then the vessel pulling smoothly

away. How sudden—the heaviness
we become. And how quickly it is over.
But if the horizon truly is
a place of arrival, a destination, then at least
you can bribe or sweet-talk the captain and come
at last to where the seam of water and sky
sweats open; to where the dead, lacquered
in their own bright alchemy, are relaxing
under umbrellas at glass-topped tables, or strolling
through the lime trees with fistfuls of petits fours
and fruits; where the serpent of eternity, locked
in its perfect circle, sleeps

in the calm shade beneath someone's chair.
You will find that the soul, having stepped at last
out of the body's darkness and into
something useful, is more fearsome, and beautiful,
than you dared to imagine. That it smells of jasmine
and warm linen. You don't have to believe

in anything; but if you imagine it,
then it could be true—even if it's only for the span
of an afternoon spent scanning the lively
etiquette of whitecaps along the horizon through binoculars,
in case they are serviettes

caught on the breeze, or a hat thrown skyward
in exuberance; a balloon let go from the heart
of the crowd, deliberately and for you.

maya

And so the ocean—the god who refuses
to enter, the god with nothing to do
but vanish and continually reappear
inside its own clothes—burns on
outside your window, and how easy it is to travel,
full circle, from the pale carnage of the water and back
to a theory of paradise. Out in the fish-spine

blue of distance the fleet is working the grounds,
and you know what it's like to drag something living
up from behind the blind face of the world
only to watch that face close over
once again before you: every day you come home

with less than you had. Going down to the shore
you find the wind on the surface of the water
smells of skin and linen smoothed flat
by the pressure of a single hand; that the ocean
has been talking so long with rocks and glass
in its mouth its breathing is ruinous and blue

as an empty bottle. Even its mercy is a terrible thing.
The ocean worries everything it owns down to nothing.

But there are days when the sunlight caught
inside the water turns the slender wall of each wave
into a house of flame. There was a time
you thought the soul was full of fire like this;
that it swung, like a lantern, high in the dark tower
of the flesh. And every grave

here faces the sea, and deep
as they are in the soil, you can hear how the god
still forms inside the bone helmets of the dead
its blue and terrible hymn. *Listen,* it sings, *you must learn
to take your life more seriously.* But what is it

I must do, you ask, to live so differently. And the only
answer is a brightness dropping down
on one knee, parting the skirts of the marram
deep in the dunes.

The Fourth Man

*I know that during that long and racking march of 36 hours over the
unnamed mountains and glaciers of South Georgia, it seemed to me often that
we were four, not three. I said nothing to my companions on the point, but
afterwards Worsley said to me, 'Boss, I had a curious feeling on the march
that there was another person with us.' Crean confessed to the same idea. One
feels 'the dearth of human words, the roughness of mortal speech' in trying to
describe things intangible. . . .*

— Ernest Shackleton

Forget what you know of the *Endurance*
assailed by ice: her crew floating blindly
inside her for months, their dogs slaughtered

one by one; the daily betrayals of panic
and despair. Courage is the body creating,
from the violent tenderness of the imagination,

a vision of itself as something possible.
What matters is how those three men kept silent,
each one submitting, in secret, to his own need.

Later, they would name the fourth one among them
Providence. But I say
it was the body's work and am certain

that each heart opened hopefully as the snow
blew loose with a hiss from under someone's boot;
when rocks, dislodged, spit away down slope;

at every shadow caught on the edge of vision.
And I am certain
that turning around to find nothing was easier to bear

than any evidence they might have discovered
walking among them. The body is not the only
terror out of which we fashion salvation, but it is

the one loneliness about which we know nothing.
It's why we make love, and dream
in pictures; it's why we make art, ravenous

for prayers in our own likeness. It's why each man
woke, off and on, to his own fiction. And believed it true.
This morning, after dreaming

in the dark, early hours and coming no closer
to this body, which I endure alone, I walked to the river
where the blue herons hung like apparitions

above their reflections and isn't this just
like the flesh, I thought: to float as the ghost of itself
above the proof of its existence.

The Rest of Us

for Roger

I'd always suspected the body was a dwelling—
a house that only children or the truly insane,
unafraid of returning to find doors
barred against them, leave at will; that the rest

of us simply stand beneath the lintel of the threshold.
Even though there are times when the foolish
among us step forward to stand
exposed beneath a sulk of sky, we never go far;

we merely look around
a bit before coming back in. Just to say
we've been there. But what of you, evicted
from the body by violence, snapped free of the flesh

for seventeen years only to return, lease in hand,
with rumours of heaven, which you remember
the way the rest of us remember childhood—
with great effort, out of sequence, one artifact

at a time: cuckoo spit, cat's eye, that perfect
cleft in the tip of a pen nib, the small carved shields
of a pair of cufflinks. The empty mouths of buckles.
The shiny boat of a shoe. And all those years

you spent in a coma add up
to a separate, complete life: a slim boy of seventeen any girl
would love for his mystery and aura of exile.
After all those years of leaning

with your lips against the locked doors of your life
you can no longer walk but have acquired a new language,
and now when you speak I swear you are speaking
with your lips against the lid

of a casket. And so heaven is built, one
thick mouthful at a time: god,
you tell me, is a casual flame burning
around the trunk of every tree and under

the shelf of every leaf, and how can I
not think about Blake, who saw angels
bleating with fire in the trees and then lived his life
with the lord's bright body caught in his throat

like a hymn. There is no heaven;
only birds and wind. And your mind
flirting with its own absence. And the late-
blooming flowers sending out dark fleets of blossom.

Roger, I think one day you just woke up
and turned over, as we all do, to face the view:
outside, summer trees and the wink of visquene
and paper among the mute, busy mouths of the leaves;

small planes ascending from a distant airfield, scaling
and then slipping inside
the grip of the wind; that a strained
film of brightness was over all things, as if the world

were the hem of a long, pale robe caught
on a branch and pulled taut.
That having been away so long, you mistook such things.
There is no god, just the limned

and tooled body of the wind at play
among the plumes of the lilac; and trust me,
there's a warmth down in the grasses, right
where they enter the soil, and it will coat

your throat like a hymn. Come, let me wheel
you out through the streets of the world,
where the rest of us live, where there are no angels;
only girls on every corner baring their beautiful limbs.

The Curator of Silence

Hail to thee, blithe Spirit!
Bird thou never wert,
That from heaven, or near it,
Pourest thy full heart
In profuse strains of unpremeditated art.
— P. B. Shelley

Over their desks they curve in a burst of sudden creation,
the crown of each head glossy as wet stone, in love

with the poet, with the bird that is hidden, like a poet,
in the light of thought. And how
difficult, when the only language they are given

is in the short, fat fingers of the twelve
waxy crayons before them; and how
beautiful that they refuse to let their visions

of the world be limited by whatever is, or is not,
on hand; that they come, one by one,
to the front of the room with their great visions—

ladders of song, great strains and stretches of singing
and the tiny bodies of the skylarks
ascending, and Shelley, hard at work, with a white

exclamation of lace at his wrists; and someone,
enthralled with how a song
peels free from the glove of a body, has rendered

this moment as the moment when the clapper
and the cup of the great bell both hang weightless and a long
resonance floats free. And after

they have all come forward she rises
up behind the fortress of her desk, her picture
held out before her like a shield, her skin

so pale you'd think it was light itself
escaping, slowly, like air, from inside her. *Here,*
she says, *is the song the bird wants to sing*

but cannot. And instead of absence, and instead
of the blankness we expect, she's drawn
a hoop of resplendent yellow. Like the breath

undressed from and abandoned by a body.
Like the chimera of a name slipped free
from the sheath of its meaning.

This is not about death: death
is a minor player. Up close, the bright
yellow wax of the song that the bird cannot sing

is so thick it is puckered and raised like a scar
and my mind moves over it like light
over water while she stands there—a small

loneliness, full of riches, the room radiant
now with a lack of singing. Through the window,
in the wind, the leaves of the lilac haggle

like tongues, but these are the only
lessons they will ever need to learn: that life
is not artifact, but aperture—a stepping into

and a falling away; that to sing is to rise
from the grave of the body. And still
say less than nothing.

Horses

We pass them being wheedled
and cajoled around small corrals, a confetti
of spit across each wide breast and the sweat
between their legs worried up into foam.
Their hooves flash in the dirt like polished bells.
We pass them as they sleep, standing up
among the dandelions and tasseled grasses
gone to seed. They enter our lives

like fragments of Eden, the place that has always
been our most difficult, elaborate dream.
And once seen—even from a freeway
when you're doing sixty, aware of your peril—
it's an effort of will to take your eyes from a horse
in a field. Grace is like that. No other animal

occupies its skin so precisely, or walks forward
so carefully, as if pushing through great hauls
of dark water, chest deep in a stiff current.
I don't believe we are meant to think about death,

even on those evenings
when a thin mist rides on the fields and their hooves
waver beneath them like votive flames. A horse

becomes its own myth and religion: out from the dark
machinery of its body something better,
and more beautiful, is always about to begin;

and if you ever need proof that it's good
to have a physical body, touching
a horse in this life is the closest you will get to it.

To catch grace off guard: a lone horse
dozing in a field, the long reach of its neck
presented to the world, its thick, lower lip fallen
away from the fence of its teeth
and there, beguiling as god's empty pocket,
pale skin of the inner mouth. Before you die
look into the eyes of a horse at least once
and discover how each is an empty room
lit by a single candle. If the gods ever come down
to walk among us, this is where they will live.
And so when a horse, seeing nothing about us

it can recognize, lowers its deep,
soft mouth to the grass and when that grass,
appearing wet in the sunlight, rises to greet it,
as if the lips of the dead were puckered skyward

for its kiss, it should be no surprise. How can we not
love an animal that spends so much of its life
with its mouth so close to the dirt. That they take,
with such tenderness, the mints
and the carrots we offer—as if the world

were ours to give—is the miracle; that they let us
            slip on the sky-blue halter and lead them
                        through the cool of the evening.

Still Life with Casaba Melon
by Jack Leonard Shadbolt

It is 1941. You are thirty-two. You know
there is something dangerous about feeling
so alive when every day there is news
of war and people lie dying and the dead

lie unburied in the streets of Europe.
And yet we die every day and sometimes
more than once and how lucky you feel, lonely
and content inside the selfishness of your art.

With your knife you have broken open
that knot of darkness at the centre
of the melon, exposing its seeds to the light.
They remind you of precious, stolen
things, of coins and cufflinks, of prayers
polished in the tube of a throat
until there is only the milk

of light, grazing. The tragedy is not
that monuments or cities or empires
vanish, but that every discovery a heart
ever makes as it travels, imprisoned, through great
vistas of feeling, goes missing. That mouths
ever close over such silence is the miracle. It is 1941.

Jack, sixty years from now I'll be forty-two.
With both feet in the twenty-first century.
Where war, as always, will lead us nowhere
except into the darkness of our own embrace.
Art is never a luxury. Look: here's a green

turning from ruin, running
up the leg of the table in a flicker of fire
with a cry like the wet crack of grass
as a shovel goes down. See, it is possible
to open the earth and hide
every fleck of the heart we'll never outgrow;
to paint, at the centre of a melon, shadows
deep enough to hold water. And the faith
of a single, unbroken brush stroke is the rope
any one of us could throw
from the window of a building, bombed

and on fire. It is 1941. You are thirty-two, creating
cold grandeur out of burning colour, moving
us through all darkness. All damage.

March 2003, and My Father
Remembers the War

Truly, I live in dark times!
. . . .
What kind of times are they, when
A talk about trees is almost a crime
Because it implies silence about so many horrors?

— Bertolt Brecht

The Beech

In my slippers and my dressing gown
I sit down to watch the war. It breaks my heart
but this time after breakfast
I'll get dressed and saunter out and sit
under the beech tree at the foot
of the garden inside the smell of compressed

grass and dirt where the cattle stand each evening
at the water trough next to the fence.

I know what it's like to lie sleepless on your back
in a copse of beech trees watching the grind
of moonlight across the shrine of every leaf,
listening to yourself dreaming and walking
back and forth inside your own death.
But I don't know how a man can be shot
right beside you and die so quietly you don't even notice.

The Madrone

I know at eleven your mother will appear
with cups of tea and thin, vanilla biscuits
fanned, like petals, around each saucer;
that we will sit down together beneath
the beech tree, as next door the slender, imported
madrone drops its bark in slow, long gestures.
For my mind it's a short
            leap from this
to skin burning off in sashes and sheets
and scarves from a body catching the light. First,

there is memory. Then, the mechanics of remembering.

The Yew

I am haunted. I dream about the handles
of axes, the polished arc of a longbow; I
know the Celts could whittle a single yew tree
down into a thousand stilettos, which were set
half buried in earth, at angles, to greet the enemy;

The Cedar

that there were tribes who braided
the bark of the cedar into clothes

and baskets and then from the heartwood
made their war canoes and arrows.

The Willow

We never could say blood is *blood*, and such failure
of mind was our true oppression. Blood
like a river! we cried; like a tie slipping loose,
like smoke, like a ribbon; and inside
those two, tiny wells that form
between the neck's quiet arc and the wing

of a collarbone when a body lies down, blood
like spills of ink. Blood in the right light
resting on a riverbank like a piece of mirror reflecting
the dark, drawn curtain of a single willow.

The Gardener

I have buried men. Imagine it. Each man at one time
a child and his mother's favourite purse reduced
to a poverty of sticks and shadows. How can we say
of the dead *there is nothing left*
when their lightness, like the high, unattainable
blue of new leaves, is our greatest burden,

when even the thinning sail of a leaf drags earthward,

when a body is left. I swear
there are nights I lie next to your mother and taste
the riddle of turned earth as she rolls over.

Look

after *The Annunciation* (fifteenth century)
from the Church of St. Marie Madeleine, Aix-en-Provence

Look, God arrives in the warp and the rattle
of thin metal: here he is, squatting with his angels
on the roof of the chapel, forcing the burnished
threads of his breath through the high, rose window,
his robe crumpled like a sheet of foil;
and if you don't look closely you think it's a hiccup
in the paint, but sliding headfirst and fully formed down
the copper chute of God's breath toward Mary
is a tiny baby with all the radiance of heaven
glazing its minuscule buttocks. And look: even God
is a victim of vanity, balancing a globe on the palm
of his hand. It's contemporary enough: don't we all
carry pictures of our children or copies of poems
in our breast pockets? And here's Gabriel
in the side chapel in his oversized cloak—no glimmer
of spandex anywhere and it's a miracle, no doubt,
to even lift off the ground when you're wearing
a cloak five sizes too large and thick as a Persian carpet.
And look: something holy wanders out of the body
to lay its burden on the world, and I don't mean
the affliction offered by God—I mean this prayer
Gabriel is uttering, the letters of each word lining
up before him in the air like a troop of insects
(even though you might assume it's graffiti
scrawled on the wall behind him—something slightly
obscene written by the watchman on his lonely
rotations through the chapel). The future depends
on what is about to happen, and that's why Mary
is locked like a target in a nimbus of subtle fire;

why Gabriel manifests language in the air, his hands
fluttering in tight, distracting gestures, terrified
she will glance upward and so turn aside
at the last moment. Mary, of course, is oblivious,
even though the pages of the book she was reading
are beginning to flutter a little in the turbulence
of God's breathing. These are the final seconds
before everything changes, for each one of us, forever—
and look, she's an ordinary woman, untroubled
by omens, thinking only of the man she is about to marry,
who right this moment is happily building cabinets
in a workshop at the bottom of his garden.

The Last Supper

It was Mary, felled by grief and on her knees
in the dirt, who mistook a man newly risen
from the dead, the only
man she'd ever really loved, for a gardener: *Sir,*
if you have carried him away, she cried, *tell me*
where you have laid him, and I will take him away.
So it's true: what we observe
sometimes betrays us. It was raining,

heavily, slowly, making the leaves of the silver ash
outside my window genuflect and bow down;
and the mirror on the dresser with its slender
dishonesty reflected and carried into the room
things from outside my field of vision: a few boats

approaching the hard, welcome arms
of the harbour, a short run of laundry
left hanging on the line next door, and the rain
closing its lips around the yellow flag and the fuchsia.
I'd always suspected the rain to be full

of such rooms and enclosures. I'd woken
jet-lagged in the late afternoon in the thin bed I'd slept
in when I was a child; woken feeling sad and lonely
even though I was neither sad

nor lonely—that was just my old self, the past
and its various disguises. I'd been dreaming
of that poet in New York City who wanders
through the busiest streets all day, recording,
in a spiral-bound, pocket-sized notebook, nothing
but the observable world. To do so, he said,
keeps him honest, and he's never seduced
by his own ideas. Strange, I'd always thought art
was a series of small deceptions
performed in the service of the truth. Already

the rain and the late afternoon were moving
toward that time of light when the quiet
benevolence that has watched us all day like a parent
turns away, and I knew I should be outside
walking, resisting any intimation of ending,
otherwise I'd feel abandoned all evening, otherwise
I'd fall back into sleep abandoned.
But it was nearly dinnertime and I

was held where I was by the music my mother made
striking her carillon of copper-bottomed saucepans,
by the breathy glide of drawer
after drawer opening then closing, opening then closing;
by the galloping of knives
across the marble cutting block.

My parents slipped me the things they insisted
they could not finish: a thin sheaf of greens,
more garnish than meal, boiled leeks and pork medallions,
a few glazed, sliced carrots, glowing
like a handful of change. And what ruined

my heart was not the thinness of my father's thighs,
or the inlay of veins around my mother's ankles;
it was not how they forgot things or remembered
what had not yet happened. It was how little

they ate; it was how my mother rallied all day
in the kitchen and then arrived at the table
with platters and great dishes that were always
almost empty. It was the way their portions became lost

in the vast, pale arenas of their plates.
If observing the world keeps us honest, what truths
do we glean watching a body we love
going into the ground? The body is both everything
and nothing.
It was the way they'd come to need so much
less of the world. And how this, perhaps, was enough.

Meditations: Tyne Cot Cemetery, Ypres

1

We shall never, as Emerson reminds us,
steer our feet clear of the grave. A day is near when I
shall exist in this world no longer and I
have no children to keep me whole in memory the way
I keep my dead now, organized under small roots
and rain. It's a long, circuitous journey to that short, final
    drop to the grave. The world is indifferent.

2

The world is indifferent, but the heart never can
be indifferent. Don't ever tell me
there are too many poems about the dead: the dead,
among whose ranks we shall one day number, outnumber
us all and should be given their due. Remember.

3

From a distance
you might believe that these white crosses are wild
swans or snow geese burning pale and clean, at rest
in the fields; or if you believe
in heaven, that they are the spittle and the teeth
of that first idea. Or that the angels, tired
of inventing miracles to hold our attention, have dropped
and left behind their wings and vestments;
. have walked, unprepared, into the mortal clasp
of history. I'm not sure what to believe.

4

I'm not sure what to believe but I'm thinking
of a shunga I saw once in which a woman
lying naked on a bamboo mat
behind a gauzy curtain is just beginning to sleep, is closing
over again after love, while her lover, having wiped

her clean, is laughing and tossing those white
tissues down all around them, over the ground.

5

Remember how Emerson, after more
than a year of searching everywhere
for the evidence of her soul, simply opened
Ellen's coffin on one of his daily sojourns
into her tomb. By then, as we all
do, he must have bartered everything and discovered
the currency of proof is small change and sometimes
not even a handful.

Boys Throwing Baseball

Your solace:
One time
you'll be relieved of the return.
      — Rolf Jacobsen

Just as I was coming out of sleep, a whole poem scrolled down in front of my
eyes. I saw it in four-line stanzas, with a closing tercet. It was beautiful, and
clear; it had a story and it made sense.

      — journal entry

There is always enough mystery to go around. Every day
even the most unlikely among us invent our stories. O,
words embedded in the dark tunnels of bones; sounds
that sit behind the tongue, waiting for the mind

to take on the shape of something we might understand.
To say it was like parchment unscrolling, or a gown
shimmying from the shoulders of a lover to reveal the blazing
wall of the backbone and that vulnerable hollow at the nape

of the neck would be wrong. It had the gravelly sound
of cheap wallpaper unraveling from ceiling to floor: something
my parents would have purchased for their small,
terraced house in the heart of England, where the factory

horns sounded at noon and the limestone facade
of the Catholic church vanished, hour by hour, into the hands
of the rain. Before me, into a room curtained against summer,
where a man in a narrow bed lay dying, walked a girl with hair

like a helmet of fire; she was carrying a book, and the hand-
picked flowers she placed on the bed outweighed
even the drag of his dying. We believe it's the silence
that's fearful, never the words; and yet whenever she stopped reading

to turn the page, he would smile. Perhaps, in that stillness
he felt his heart stop searching for instructions
on how to live. By the sixth stanza she'd left him, the book
splayed open on the nightstand, and small, black

beetles were emerging, finally, from the failing petals
of the flowers. And that's when we heard the boys outside: the soft,
sexual grunt of release, the felt arc of something hard
passing though air; then that perfect tang

as a ball smacked home, solidly, into a glove. That's when
I sank into the place she had vacated, and we listened to that rhythm
of release and return and to the stillness between
that must sometimes pass for language. I got up

eventually but was with him all day feeling the pure
silence of the ball's trajectory in the leaf-guarded street, waiting
for the sound of that one return we never hear arrive.

Epitaph on Interstate 80, Nevada

A miracle, just take a look around:
the inescapable earth.

    — Wisława Szymborska

The world is a grave. With all its exits barred. The only
station available is Pilgrim Radio, whose preachers tell you of your need
for penance and salvation and attempt to convince you that the body
is never worth it. Even though you know the loneliness
you feel in the landscape is only an echo of the body's grave
and specific sadness, you listen: light connecting to the dirt

with a sigh, like the blade of a guillotine; the dead dissolving into dirt.
Fields the size of small countries. Dead cattle. The rest of the herd only
grazing happily, brushing up against the pockets and the graves
of their bodies. Even if, the preachers tell you, you succumb to need
and find someone lovely enough to tempt you out of loneliness
into longing, you can still turn away from the pleasures of the body

and find your way back into the sufferings of the body
by striking a match and slipping your fingers into the flame. The dirt
of the world drifts through the rooms of the heart. What other loneliness
do you need: the world is a grave, it is the mind's only
mirror. The dead are with you, part of the journey: smears of hunger
    and need
on the tarmac; blisters of flesh in the tread of a tire. Small, open graves.

And those preachers who regard the flesh as nothing but a grave,
who burn, literally, because of lust and beauty; men for whom the body
is a coffin inside which the heart travels and kneads,
day after day, chamber by chamber, the compost and flotsam and dirt
of its own desires; men for whom the soul is a new coin, the only
one not minted for spending (such thrift, surely, buys nothing but
    loneliness),

what would they make, I wonder, of your loneliness
if they knew how it had you kneeling now, as if beside a grave,
next to a doe in the grass by the side of the road; how it's only
in death that her tongue swooning from her mouth makes a bridge
     between her body
and the dirt;
how, for the keys you carried once—prayers and pleading—you have
     no need.

When you finally rise there are two slight depressions kneed
into the grass and you discover here the real pennant of loneliness—
the flensed skin of a doe's back trailing its sash against the dirt;
the sudden flare of fascia like nothing you'd imagined about the grave,
but like the lining of a jacket a woman might throw, casually, about
     her body
when stepping out in strapless ball gown with her lover, the only

man she'll ever need, even after they have sunk her, finally, into her
     grave.
However you look at it, the loneliness of the world begins in the body.
And the body earns its dirt, and all its delight, in this world only.

Giving It Away

There are few things I'd keep: an antique
locket with my picture inside it and a mixture
of herbs the catalogue touted as *Protection;* a thimble

that belonged to my mother, the skull
of a crow, my father's dog tags. Even so, there is much
I can live without. And sometimes it feels

that even my memories belong
to everyone else: my lovers,
the colic of their mouths all over me year

after year, who took from me, quietly,
things I never knew I had; that stranger whose hand I let slip
into my jeans on the Dublin ferry

when I was sixteen. Especially him. And earlier,
my parents with their clamorous need.
The world robs us like this until

almost nothing is left. And some of us choose
to give away even that: a tin cup exhumed
from the newly turned flowerbeds; poems

salvaged from the peelings and coffee grounds;
seed pods and the hollow stems of grasses. The dark,
polished pockets of a human heart. Whatever shape

emptiness finally arrives in.

The Silver Vase

written after a high school residency, Western Minnesota

Loveliness, he wrote, *is like an aging shed*
in the forest: Tyler Joel Rakowski, first row,
second from the left, sliding round in his chair
as if he had grease on the seat of his trousers
to stare at Tanya Engler in the back corner
by the bookcase, where all week
she made her poems, ordering the titles of novels
in some magical arrangement all her own
right down the middle of the page. Wild
with loneliness. Like wind that's come a long way.
Find me the word, I'd told them, *to describe what collects*
in the corners of your heart. And I'm sure
it was *loneliness* he meant, but who among us

would ever refuse a slip like that.
And the next day it is snowing,
a white fugue slicking the world to a new thing.
And the day after that. *Let the poem be strange,*
I say, *mysterious; let it hold everything*
you don't want to know about your life.
They write about death,
their faces floating like moons over the dark
finish of their desks. A few miles west
and it's South Dakota and what use is mystery.
Imagine you're a tourist and give yourself
one thing to take home. They choose
the steady hiss of wind along the border
of a field; the dry cough of freight
linking in the rail yards at night;
the way a brother vanished
in the darkness of winter. For which
there is no relief. *Loveliness,* he wrote,

is like a silver vase, untarnished and whole.
And they write from the unspoiled world

of the body, which they will know only briefly
for what it is before choosing to remember
the bright taste of finitude during their first sex
as its opposite. And are led astray
by the bleak neon of the spirit. *Loveliness,*
he wrote, *is like a tide rushing over me.*
It is March, but the girls, unreadable, beautifully
adrift, wear skirts and open sandals; they discuss
the agony of love as if it's a rare thing while the boys

wait, growing into their hands, which are the large
hands of men, which they place on their desktops
while I talk. *No matter where I turn,*
he wrote, *or how many doors I shut*
behind me, it's always there. And when I leave

I don't get far: a storm hauling in
from South Dakota keeps me on the shoulder
with the engine running. I lean back
into the calm luminosity. And, yes, our lives
are short. But I'm not thinking about death;
I'm thinking about how, without shadow, under
a certain democracy of light, all things
turn silver. You can call it loveliness
or loneliness: if we are lucky,
they're the same thing. And I like how it feels.
I close my eyes, he wrote, *as tight*
as they go, and I can see.

Elegy for Mumbai

The British artist Damien Hirst has found controversy again. This time it is not for his pickled sheep or sharks floating in tanks of formaldehyde, but for a new piece, "Amazing Revelations," a triangular collage made of thousands of dismembered butterfly wings.

— *New York Times*, August 19, 2003

These are not the beauties of our childhoods—
those common beauties we painted, open-
winged on their favourite flowers,
their native landscapes in the background marching
away: Mourning Cloak, Brimstone,
Adonis Blue. But there are voices
everywhere: wings like mouths held open
around a single hue—thalo,
manganese, Prussian, cerulean—blues
that slip out of us when we
are sleeping, and here and there a green
so fanciful it's like a door left open under the grass.
Such beauty is the aftermath
of terrible violence. There are wings
here with hems of copper that are burning, slightly,
like the troubled air around a moving
bullet and my thoughts
wander to Audubon in long, silk stockings
and fancy satin breeches shooting
his way through Pennsylvania in the name of art,
passing wires through the dead
bodies of birds before posing each
one carefully and taking up his palette and his brushes
to prove that death, not art,

imitates life. Butterflies, it is said, release
faint odours; among them, red clover and fresh honey.

In my mind there are bevies of schoolboys
racing every Friday after class
to the artist's greenhouse where the weekly,
afternoon shipment has been released.
Beneath their clothes, these boys
are hairless, unmuscled; they toss
their schoolbooks and satchels down
on the grass. Beyond the greenhouse
the lawns are manicured and formal—
no emotion anywhere and, O, I think,
let a handful of girls slip
through the green nimbus of the lilac, break
from the clasp of leaf light into
the open, let them be wearing gingham skirts
and white blouses; let those boys feel love's soft knock
on the breastbone and hesitate only
a moment before turning away from their terrible
work. Let them turn away from their terrible work.
But it will not happen. I am here
in a gallery in a city in the civilized
world where even the view
through the window is like a painting, albeit
a Sunday afternoon by Seurat with sunbathers
scattered like sweets on the grass, and a river
releasing then replacing its own long body, and a dog,
trailing its leash, running free
through the park. And before me this wall
of shimmering evidence—wings
like flakes of mica, like chips of spruce
bark and Roman tile, like face cards and stolen
coats of coloured dust. How many ways
can there possibly be to separate
wings from a body? Wings

like snips of silk. Dresses
too beautiful to wear. I should, I know,

be thinking about the slag heaps of shoes at Chelmno
and Auschwitz, at Sobibor and Treblinka;
about the skulls gathered up
like stones from the soils of Rwanda, the soils
of Bosnia, from the soils of El Salvador and
Cambodia; about the victims of wars in eight out of every
ten countries I can name, and how
a hundred, a thousand, ten thousand, a million
can be herded to a common fate and yet
each death be different. But all I can think
of is how, only yesterday, in the aftermath
of a bomb blast at a market in Mumbai,
among the strewn, charred wreckage

and shredded bodies, rescuers found other debris—whole
pineapples, oranges, sweet limes.

Private Mythology

Lost: large piece of green canvas.
— notice in the local newspaper,
  Moose Lake, Minnesota

I smile about it over hash browns
and a three-egg omelette, surrounded
by folk art and gingham and the high
strafe of conversation; yet who really knows,
I think, the importance and the value we assign
to the dross and the mementos of a life?
and I develop my own private
mythology in which that canvas, the arena
of your outdoor lovemaking, was opened
fold by fold, with quiet ritual, over the insects
and the grasses. I want its loss
to have been prolonged and gradual: a drawn-
out lifting from the back of your pickup,
which you drove too fast on a straight, gravel road
so remote the radio faded in and out of static
and the only steady music was a sigh
deep in the corn, close to the roots. The undertow
of the wind pulling through it. And had you
glanced up into the rearview mirror
you'd have seen your magical canvas unfurling
over the fields. But she was as close to you
as she could get. It was her hip against yours

all the way home. I know how it is: you spell it out
to the clerk at the local paper and start
wrestling through the pale wings of the morning
edition to the right page. Each day
so many things go missing. Each day
at least one will be found. And you are among

those blessed with fortune because one morning
the phone will ring or you'll discover
on page sixteen, inside a tight
basket of type, that someone has at last recovered
the scrap of life you misplaced.
You are a local traveller.
You will not drive far. It will only feel
like crossing a continent without directions, driving
minor highways devoid of road signs through countries
where the petrol stations carry no maps
and sell only postcards and cigarettes
and travel sweets dusted with sugar.

Then, when the door finally opens,
you'll reach forward, smiling wildly, to claim
what is yours. It won't feel like a miracle—
but your parents, who you'd thought beyond reach
in the new world of the grave, will be there;
and that one, suede boot, lost when your old,
leather case snapped open in the belly of a plane;
and the light of a certain afternoon in August
when a lover, your first, sailed
aground quietly against the body of another man.
How far you did or did not travel to be here

will matter no longer. Because here you are.
And the world will be turning the corner
into nightfall, because in all the best stories
the traveller stands in darkness at the threshold
and takes back, by the armful, everything
that was once believed lost for good.

Naming the World

I remember what it felt like naming
the world, setting the feet of each
word carefully on the faint blue lines
of the page; how the arms
of an *O* came together, like a door
closing, like a heart shutting down; how lower-
case *g* could release me, with a flourish,
from the hook of its tail, like my father's
arms sending me skyward on a swing,
thin legs and scuffed shoes over
my head, a sudden jigsaw of leaves
and sky and pigeons launching out
over the park on a firm applause
of wings. Then the fall back, earthward,
into those same arms. I remember

the miracle of building, with my own
hand, the roof of a letter—dome
of a bird's skull, patina of light on wet bone.
Back then I thought god
had formed the names of the animals
over and over in the dirt. Until
they had risen up. And he'd let them go. I
was shamed by the emptiness
inside my own name, by the headstone
of each downstroke, by how easily I
could be debrided by that pale pink nipple
of rubber on the end of a pencil.
Put it into words we were told,
as if language were a bucket, a mouth,
a light-blue shirt. Fist. Inkwell. Bag
of tricks. The complete, white
fire that was the body of a swan
down in the reeds by the river.

Locket, pencil case, the green lamp
of a leaf. Or those rooms inside the rain
we walked though all day without entering.
Why, when there is so little life
to go around, do we still run out of places
to keep it and what else should we do
with the words we tear from the currents
of a poem but let them go? Such tenderness
and generosity even I can manage: see,
there are sentiments about death
that I have chased to the sill
of an open window; and *the locked*
slaughterhouse of the heart I have set adrift
in a rowboat without any oars, in which
it will float, unnoticed, out
between the jaws of the harbour. I will carry
that *brittle, bright hunger on which*
we float out into the forest and release it
back into the earth; and, just in case,

the animal that ignites within the body
I will not separate from the body. Just in case,
I will send them forward together.

The Dream in Broad Daylight

I walk beneath the trees through a house
of green fire, down across the rocks and the locked,
blue closets of the mussels to where the sockeye
are bottlenecked at the mouth of the river
under the great footfall of the sun,
in water canorous with their desire.

They have travelled, without choice, for years,
back to the salmagundi of leaf-light and shadow
in the river's rills and braids, where the waters
still taste like the drawn shock of their first breathings,
like the flesh of their parents, of blood
and milt and precious metals.

I could walk across the bay on the raft they make
with the fire and spackle of their bodies, and it's easy
to see how two of them in the hands of a prophet
once satisfied us in such numbers.
There are many kinds of hunger,

and slipping into water is like coming home,
to great welcome, after an argument,
so in my mask and fins and my brand-new skin
I swim through their ranks of flame. I tell you

there is something immense—like the dark
inside mirrors and cathedrals, like a forest
seen at night from a train—inside the eyes of fish;

that behind the armoured portal of every
single gill plate winks the luminous, wistful signal
of the gills like something partly forbidden—glints,
perhaps, and glimpses of the dead in their ceaseless vigils
behind every one of a thousand doors

standing suddenly ajar. When there's nothing
in the world to write about, said Rilke, we must write
about our dreams and fears. But what happens if the world

itself is our dream. And our fear. And our fear
is that we vanish like they do—dreaming of home,
mouthing for air, driven, starving, dressed
in crimson. One among many. Like a luff
of radiance when the wind turns
towards shore at evening. And our dream, of course,
is the same.

Observing the Afterlife

Even when you give them up, the promises appear
everywhere. There's one on that open curve
just across the Mississippi on 94, between the exits
for Cleveland and Vandalia: *Crown Royal,* it says;
Heaven On Earth, and that massive bottle emerges
like a woman's body from its purple robes. This is a leap
I can't fathom until I think about sex and the way men
undress—simply, undoing buttons, opening their shirts
like curtains in a challenge

to the waiting world. But a woman will slide
halfway out of her dress and stand there, quiet
and anonymous, the thin fabric rucked casually
around her waist. I would tell this to a friend

who drinks to bypass the dark work of prayer. Who travels
through the bodies of women to locate the soul.
Afraid someone will find it before him and take it
mouthful by mouthful, piece by piece.
But it would make no difference. Every morning

it catches him at that long red light on Marshall,
where he is offered something
Better Than Real Life. It breaks him apart,
this promise pouring out like a mudslide into tumblers
the size of swimming pools, and he fills those glasses
with bodies: a weekend barbecue gone berserk
where the passion between people married
to other people moves into a wordless
fuck in a back room with the windows open, the fresh

taste of cut grass on everything. Many of us
have already gone far enough
inside that proffered world and know that the soul is ordinary
and domestic, something we have gathered up
without a second thought and saved, like an odd bead
or a button, like a stamp that arrives into our hands
unmarked. Like a piece of string—never
the whole skein, which is useful and complex,
but a small length, frayed at each end.
And this is what he cannot bear: a world where even
death is mundane and without promise.

Where a woman rising out of her clothes is simply a woman
rising out of her clothes.

Crow

The world follows us
into our dreams (what else are dreams; where else
can the world go). It followed me into the forest

of first one dream, then another, calling,
always, from a branch in the darkness
over my left shoulder. And you know
how it is in a forest after dark:
each space in the canopy an open window
on the cold indifferent reach of the void. Silent.
Without end. They were soft calls,

uttered back to back, familiar (intimate, even)
like layers of smoke in a barroom, like cards
in a fast deal skimming the dark
lake of a varnished table, like the hands
of a labourer snagging on silk. I thought

it was simply my fear of middle age
because the silk throat of youth had closed
at last on its cat-mouth pinks and vermilions;
or a growing obsession with omens
and portents, where hints of death
in a dream mean the worldly, literal
demise of the body from which the soul will open
like a blue umbrella—until I recognized
something familiar from childhood: a residue—
not a taste or an odour, but an aftermath
of knowledge sighing across the mind

like fine ash. Death, is it not true
you are everyone's lover; the ultimate
philanderer and our one, true heritage, packed
at birth into the suitcase of every cell. From eternity
we come forward, parting the curtains
of our mothers' bodies, but it's you we turn
to in our cribs when we lie down; and you
follow each of us like a voyeur after dark in a small town
moving from one lit window to another.
I have made it my business to know
your disguises and am used to you arriving dressed
in your mantle of oil and feathers to lean
against the curve of the skull behind my left ear.
And it was your voice I heard, was it not—that sibilant
undertow spliced through my mother's whispers
as she waded through the darkness of the nursery
when I was weeping and could not sleep: *hush now,*
hush, I'm here. I'm here. And in each house along the street

the same singing, and in each street of the city,
and in every city. All over the earth. Even the mind

is darkness without shape
until something speaks or sings. (And I opened my arms,
did I not, and reached out, toward that singing.)

The Cherry Picker

This was an intimacy I had not expected: slipping
my body into his working clothes, into the pellucid
kick of loneliness and sweat and an emptiness
that felt like fear. Even the snaps were too large.
I fastened them, claiming all

his losses. His hands, as he helped me
over the rail onto the platform, were hard
and relevant against the back of my thigh and
I wondered then if he were married. It was raining

and the trees were a green you imagine existing
only as a dream inside the skulls
of birds. The cuffs of his jacket
fell level with my knees; *McGRAFF* it said
across the back in wide, reflective letters.

When we rose from the world, from the up-turned
faces of the firemen below, I lost, but not
all at once, the sulkiness of someone's lower lip; the scar
above another's eye—that raised

nick in the hair of an eyebrow a reminder
of how the body gets damaged in deep
and common ways. All around, the trees fell away
to a green indifference. I watched his hands.
When he spoke it was about the moodiness

of hydraulics, about the lightness of touch it takes
sometimes to get work done—the flirtation
so brave, it was a luxury
I refused, and yet I wanted to reach out

through the permission he gave and touch
his arm; say, *listen, do you hear that?*
because birds were flying under us, their songs
sounding wrong; I wanted to pull his head down
close to mine and make him listen

to the rain, having come so far to reach us,
sounding important against the fabric of his jacket;
to our breath, having come further still,
catching, loud and significant,

beneath the helmet's wide rim. I wanted him
to pay attention to what there is; to the sudden
lust you can feel for a stranger making its small
noises against the back of your throat
because of how he smiles whenever you grip

the rail of the cherry picker as it bounces,
slightly, high over the car park; how, when he asks,
looking down, *have you had enough?* you notice
the clean, perfect crescents of his fingernails, rain

shining in the hair at the nape of his neck, the dark
stigmata the wet rail has made
across the front of his trousers. It's details like this
that change a life. So you look down, away,
toward that privacy the trees create

around themselves, in sunlight, with their leaves,
and say, before you can touch him, *yes.*

Aurelia aurita

I dream of an art so transparent that you can look through it and see the world.

— Stanley Kunitz

They bloomed, or so it seemed, one night
each summer and rode, on the tide's insistence,
through the harbour by the thousand until

the loneliness of our first home from whose
dark, unwalled room we are forever exiled
became intimate as they hung there dressed

in their fringed, sheer skirts. And inside each bell,
the four, pale loops of the gonads like the straps
of cheap, shiny handbags, wishbones

and stirrups, thin bracelets of lilac plastic.
I was used to the window the shadow
of a body made—the window of my own reflection

on the water through which I could gaze
and discover the barnacles'
tall, white nipples and crabs in their riot gear

of red ochre. But I'd never seen
a body like that: a body that was itself
like a window. If you wanted to touch, to get level

with their soft crowding, there were places—
and that is where he found me, out
by the whitewashed limb of the lighthouse, down

on the lowest rocks of the breakwater,
on my knees. I saw the sudden up-
rush of hair on his torso and the blind,

dark eye through which he was joined once
to his mother and, until he bent down to gather
one of those shining domes up from the water,

he was, truly, the most beautiful
of things. His teeth were a swath
of heaven. Its body

was in the air for the briefest moment, the water
trailing behind it like strings of spit, and it sang
like a dish, like a crown, like a skull-

cap of glass, and then, against stone, it sang
like a hand coming down, hard,
on wet skin: no echo, no resonance—just one

surface meeting another and small, efficient pieces
of fire all around on the rocks. Day after day
I went back until the tide had taken

all evidence away. Now there's a dream I keep having
in which god ruins everything, hurling the world
against the boulders of a breakwater, filling

the air with stivers of spittle and avulsed fire.
In my dream the harbour is a mattress
of tasseled bodies, each one branded

with hoofprints, as if an army had ridden
in great numbers across the vast, unboned body
of the ocean; and I am standing

at god's right hand, there's the frottage of sunlight
on water, the smell of creosote and diesel,
and when I wake it is always that moment

right before dawn when the world—from the small, bone
buttons on the dress of the wind, to the heart,
with its four, unswept rooms—is pulled

back into the curve, is held in
against the slick, kind scoop of the wave
before the day, literally, breaks.

I make coffee by touch in the darkness.
The sudden blister of birdsong the only fire.

One Year of Not Drinking:
A Letter at Thanksgiving

November. And that glare comes back, each evening,
into the leafless branches of the cottonwood.
They are so still. I love how light ignites
trees from the inside. These
are moments so close to happiness, so obvious,
that the world has them masked in sadness.
I discover I love sparrows for their urban,
melancholy song, for how it echoes
between buildings—little chips of sound
like stones knocking together.
I catch a flicker of wings in the branches.
The real business of this world is not large.
And I wait each day like this for evening as if
it were the promise of god, because all my life
I've been waiting to believe in something:
as a girl I watched black and white classics
in which tall, dramatic women in strapless dresses
were cheated in love and stayed drunk all day, drifting,
with heavy-bottomed tumblers,
through mansions of eternal evening
sunlight, their lipstick always perfect, their rings
and bracelets chiming against the glass while I sat
in the burdened loneliness of my childhood,
craving forward, waiting to grow up and be tortured
in love, glamorously drunk all day, my lover in bed
with someone else. Already I was relishing
the inevitable: the fight when the lover returns,
the hurled glass and my hair unfastening,
the shadow of my cleavage never
quite deep enough to seem wanton. Today,
your letter arrived: *sweet girl*, you wrote,
do not despair; answers, if there are
answers, will come like children into your arms,
or they will continue to hide in the tall

grasses like the seabirds they really are;
and I want to tell you, now, how the curlews
move through the knee-high grass in that field
behind my parents' house, and how, when you stand
at the window watching each blade tilt
in the light, you can't tell if it's wind or the birds
moving things until they rise in a flock, surprised
by themselves, and balk away
over the inlet. Until that moment, you weren't
even sure they were there at all, even though
the promise that they might have been
was with you as you stood at the window, your hands
against the cold metal of the sink, the boiler
firing in the room next door with a wheeze of air.
Their disappearance will leave you abandoned,
though you can't say why.
These days in every novel I read I get stuck
in those scenes where the characters drink
without consequence. Often it's only a sentence or two,
but I take that life, over and over, into my own.
At that window in my parents' house with nothing
but the wind tugging among the grasses,
you can spend all day watching the clouds
move their shadows over the hills.
Some small, significant possibility for joy shuts down
when you feel a landscape pass out of sunlight into shade.
The most beautiful thing is that anything is left at all.

The Poet in Reflection

I emerge from the mind's
cave into the worse darkness
outside, where things pass and
the Lord is in none of them.
                    — R. S. Thomas

I discover myself at last: a woman reflected
in a picture window, bent over
her work in a circle of light, unarmed, struggling
to place one lasting thing at the threshold
of her vanishing. Behind her,

the stairs dissolve upward into darkness
and the long hall fades
into shadow. There's a basket of birch bark
piled high with lake rocks and driftwood; two
marble doves on the mantle, their wings
unlocked in a premise of flight; and the pelt
of an animal impossible to name,
removed, as it is, from the bossy
delight of the body, from the happiness that gives us
our recognizable form. The whole night leans

against the window and the lake beyond
is forgotten until, far out on the water, lights
appear: lakers, loaded with taconite, on their way
to Detroit, or Windsor, Ontario. And before her,

behind the white door of the page, the darkness
of the mind before it thought itself into existence.

And how long does it take those ships to travel
from one shore to another, weighed down
with evidence of a previous darkness, deeper,
even, than the one they ply through? Long
enough. Long enough.

Ars Poetica

As if it could save my life. And it might.
For the dead inside the hem of the earth.
For the dead dismissed in cascades and scarves of ash.
Over fields and great bodies of water. Or resting
on a shelf inside the bud of an urn.

For those less ash than nuggets and snippets of bone.
For those not found.
For those not yet born, at rest
in the imagination's deepest pocket with the harmless,
unstrung vertebrae of the gods. Waiting

for the lusts and the mistakes of the living
to give them form. And so to the living.
For the living. For us. With our dead and our deities. For us,
with our lips against the tiny headstones we make each time
we put our soft hands together in prayer.

A Winter Portrait of My Neighbour George

No wind and by evening
narrow walls of snow were balanced along
the branches of every tree.
All afternoon, the crows patrolling
the garden had driven the songbirds
from that rough-cut table under
the cottonwood where George had strewn
his cornucopia of bacon fat and seeds.

It happened quickly and all at once: the cat
pouring under the fence to a sharp
rataplan of calls, the spume
of powder and feathers, the inaudible percussion
of two small bodies meeting; then George and I
rushing out in our slippers, intent on salvation.
Until it grew completely dark

we shadowed that bird as it ploughed
in wild troughs around the garden;
if we were coaxing, I couldn't tell, but our lips
formed sounds in such a way
it made me think we were singing. All night
that bird kept crying from the garden
and from high in the darkness, the answering
cries of assurance. And then, next morning,
those crows who'd stayed awake in the strange
roost of the cottonwood disbanded,
slowly, in groups of twos and threes,
and it was well past dawn before the last
ones finally lifted, darker, it seemed,
and more burdened than the rest.
All day that bird abandoned in the garden
called intermittently, and then fell silent.
All day I wrote my poems, rising out

of and looking back upon the body
with no misgivings about where I belonged:
it is good, I wrote, *to have a physical body;*
this way the spirits we have
might enjoy each other. I was even happy
with how abstractions arrived at the truth.
But George knows abandonment
is not an abstraction: one long winter
he'd slept on the floor of his living room listening
to his dying mother bartering with the saints
and the Virgin in his double bed. He'd slept
with his head against the wall so he would hear
her calling. She'd died calling out
his nickname, a word unheard since he'd turned
fifteen, when she thought him a man and therefore
beyond her. He'd heard the pleading
in her, been shocked by how erotic one word
could feel; and even though what she'd asked
for had seemed such a small thing, he'd turned
away from the wall and done nothing.

Crows

I saw that strange blend of softness
and brittle energy in the shattered wing,

and the blue that floated beneath the surface
of its feathers—sometimes the flesh is a mirror

but it's never this world that's reflected.
There was nothing on the beach of interest

except this body. As I moved away
they came down, out of the trees—after the first,

an avalanche—to stand fussing
in a circle around their dead companion.

They were there until the tide came in,
lifted that broken body up on its hem, turned,

and floated it out—an untidy blackness riding
into view, then vanishing, with each swell.

All they did was wait there. Keeping vigil.
That's all. There are times when this world

is just enough like paradise.

Notes

"*maya.*" *Maya* is the Hindu belief that this world is an illusion.

"*Still Life with Casaba Melon* by Jack Leonard Shadbolt." The phrase "cold grandeur out of burning colour" is from *Jack Shadbolt* by Scott Watson (Vancouver: Douglas & McIntyre, 1990).

"Meditations: Tyne Cot Cemetery, Ypres." Tyne Cot Cemetery, situated to the northwest of the Belgian town of Ypres, is the biggest cemetery of British war graves of World War I. It contains nearly 12,000 graves and a memorial to over 35,000 men who are recorded as missing with no known grave.

"Shunga," or "images of spring," are erotic polychrome engravings painted by the masters of the Japanese Ukiyo-e school during the seventeenth, eighteenth, and nineteenth centuries. The shunga served as illustrations for love novels, instructive albums for young wives, and even as lucky charms for warriors.

"*Aurelia aurita.*" The *Aurelia aurita* (also known as the Moon Jellyfish) is an almost colourless jellyfish with four, horseshoe-shaped gonads visible in the shallow bell. *Aurelia* with purple or pink gonads are males; those with yellow gonads are females. This particular species floats near the surface and is often encountered in huge swarms.